The Romance of Home

The Romance of Home

HOUSES BY MOHON INTERIORS

Marcus Mohon

with Kyle Hoepner

RIZZOLI
NEW YORK

New York · Paris · London · Milan

To the generation before, who gave us everything:
Dan and Manon Mohon and Oliver and Mary Alice Deike.

And to the generation after us, for whom
we hope to do the same: Mason and Tracy, Gray, Reed,
Bliss, little Mason, and those still to come.

CONTENTS

A Journey Toward Home 8

Timeless Vision 14
Sanctuary 38
Taken Away 62
New Life 86
Belonging 112
Imparting Identity 126
A Sheltered Place 146
Good to Great 166
Leap of Faith 184
A Frame for Beauty 198
Making It Personal 222

Acknowledgments 238
Credits 240

a Journey toward Home

The idea of *home*, for me, has always been one of joy, celebration, fellowship, and comfort. Maybe that's why I am always, in a sense, trying to make my way back there. When I was younger, the vision was one of nostalgia, of longing: I was looking to recapture the home of my youth (it was a really great one). Now, years later, my deepest impulse is to put together places of love, beauty, and security for my wife, Autumn, our four children, and the next generations of our family. And when I'm designing for my clients, the same motivation is in play.

With this in mind, design becomes much more than a matter of making rooms look nice. My not-so-secret wish is to devise settings in which my clients can lead their ideal lives. If, as the ancient Greek philosophers thought, beauty is connected to the emotions, to goodness, and to truth, then being surrounded by beauty can help anchor us so that we are buoyed, strengthened, encouraged. Our environment affects how we think and feel, and therefore influences how we behave. Where would that be more the case than at home?

SEEING WITH THE HAND

Especially in a time when our awareness is constantly saturated with imagery—on television, on social media, in shelter magazines, in books like this one—it's easy to assume that achieving style merely means assembling the right elements in the right combinations, based on the models that are all around us. The best design, however, starts from a more fundamental level and is about pure *creation*: inventing and fabricating exactly what is needed to fit a particular location, and a particular family, perfectly.

Sketches and watercolor renderings have become incredibly important to my process of working with clients for just that reason. The act of drawing, of simply putting pencil to paper, engages the imagination and unleashes visionary power. Drawing brings unseen things closer to reality, allowing you to truly picture a space and its contents

from the ground up, independent of anything you may already have come across on Instagram or in a showroom. When clients and I meet to talk about what we should do in a home, rather than going away and mapping out a scheme to present later, I'll often sketch possibilities right there with them, so they can react in real time. It helps them see our emerging concept instantly and guides their understanding of where we are headed.

Starting from a blank page is also why custom work is such a big part of Mohon Interiors projects. A sconce of the specific profile we want or a sofa having precisely the right silhouette, scale, and gracefully curved arm may not exist in the marketplace—so we'll start visualizing those items as we sit together rather than trying to search for a commercial product that's only approximately suitable. All artists and designers are influenced by the past, of course, yet conjuring up a result that's legitimately fresh, completely personal, and one of a kind is the intent—an objective far removed from simply copying others or making do with what you can buy.

A QUEST FOR TIMELESSNESS

Living and working in Austin, Texas, has underscored for me the need many people have for homes that can function as havens of stability in addition to providing shelter. The city has grown hugely in recent decades, thrusting up in the center and spreading out into the encircling Hill Country as the population has surged. Such a quick pace of change can generate a corresponding hunger for serenity and for things that will last—and the houses we've made for our clients invariably have a timeless quality to them. Each one transports its occupants to a romantic destination far removed from day-to-day concerns.

Timeless means that we never design a room or a residence to be cool or trendy. If a living environment is going to reflect your essence, it won't be something that changes every season, like a pair of loafers. It will have consistency and permanence, in the way your most essential personal tastes do over the course of your lifetime. That may be why so many of our projects have a Mediterranean ambience: the region that includes Greece, Italy, and southern France has an enduring hold on our imaginations as the wellspring of classical Western culture. Modernity there hasn't displaced history; the two coexist in a vibrant partnership. Drawing on that heritage, I employ classical proportions, motifs, and materials to construct sites where contemporary American lives can be lived.

For a house to genuinely embrace and nurture its inhabitants, it must always be approachable, no matter how grand. Too much perfection, and the rooms can seem forbidding. We are careful to include those sheltered nooks and moments of respite that give you a spot to settle and catch your breath. Private spaces deserve the same degree of investment and attention as public ones—after all, they're where you'll be spending the majority of your time. I once had a client ask, "Do we really need draperies in the back hallway?" My response: "Absolutely! This is how *you* enter your house every day."

Layers of complexity ensure that a home will maintain its interest and continue to delight over the long term. Balances of opposing decorative elements—light versus dark, sculptural paired with streamlined, the elegant juxtaposed against the humble—all add to the enchantment. Rhymes and repetitions of weight and shape and color and texture provide a stabilizing web of coherence, although I invariably include a few elements that are unexpected or may not at first appear as if they "belong." You might think of the technique as comparable to the way a gifted cook prepares a stew or ratatouille: throw the right blend of ingredients into the pot—along with a touch of spice—and it will cook down to form a delicious harmony. (And just as a dish can be even better after a day or two in the fridge, our goal is for a Mohon Interiors' home to only grow richer with time.)

OUR HOPE FOR HOME

If a home is about living your best life, it must support you through both your ups and your downs. It's where gatherings take place—holidays spent with all the relatives, your children's first birthdays, dinner parties for dear friends—and it's where you can kick back with a glass of wine and your favorite book. It's the refuge where you can heal and regain your footing in times of mourning and loss. It's where your personal history is written, those moments that will linger in memory decades down the line.

My role is to serve as a torchbearer, lighting my clients' path on our journey of discovery. The job includes a bit of archaeology, helping people unearth what they love, and some psychology, figuring out what makes their hearts beat faster. But with pencil and watercolors in hand, we set out to dream up the kind of dwelling—soulful, sophisticated, gracious, hospitable—that will elevate its owners and provide pleasure for anyone who visits. Design is the tool we use to help our clients end up in a place where they can live to their fullest potential. It's the tool we use to bring them home.

Timeless Vision

Timelessness is a quality I think about a lot, and I want to give every house I design an aura of permanence. Things that last make us feel secure, bringing contentment—even a sense of hope—through their promise of longevity. When clients of mine acquired this Spanish-inflected dwelling in the Pacific Palisades neighborhood of Los Angeles, it already had a good bit of that feeling going for it. Perched on a hillside and equipped with a broad rear terrace overlooking the ocean, the structure boasted generous, well-proportioned spaces, lovely ironwork, and eye-catching floors of waxed terra-cotta tile laid in a herringbone pattern. We had no reason to reinvent the wheel for the interiors. Our task, instead, was a matter of building on the existing foundation of solid traditional architecture and a showstopping view to add layers of graciousness and comfort as well as tailor the residence to the specific wishes of its new owners.

When I refer to *timelessness*, though, I don't mean putting together textbook re-creations of antique fashions, like dusty period rooms in a museum. My goal is a stylistic mix, rooted in good principles of design, that will endure and not be dated a few years down the road. The blend can include recent pieces just as much as those that recall earlier eras. We're now at a point where modernism from the twentieth century is folded into the classics—after all, some of that furniture is being sold as antique these days. As a result, a combination such as the one you see in this home's foyer—a stone table that could seemingly have been carved centuries ago in Italy juxtaposed with a lamp descended from French modernism, a well-used baroque candlestick, and a contemporary painting—can appear ageless, not trendy.

Contrast quickly emerged as another primary ingredient in the project. The home's architecture already incorporated strong oppositions between light and dark; we therefore tried to work with that architecture and engineer our interventions to match.

OPPOSITE: Richness, refinement, relaxation, and comfort were all key objectives in the development of this home on the Southern California coast, and the trick was to achieve a balance that didn't lean too far in one direction or another. Sketching ideas for the living room, I imagined an assembly of classic silhouettes clothed in subtle textures and tied together through the consistent repetition of shapes.

Because an element like the tile floor, handsome as it was, could get out of control quite quickly, we used light, unpatterned rugs and a pale tonal palette for most of the furnishings, plus enough splashes of deep brown to keep things grounded. We also kept the custom upholstery simple in attitude despite some dramatic profiles. Against this background, more-intense items could stand out instead of getting lost in visual clutter. Weighty colors or bold statements like a carved fireplace or iron chandelier require relief; there has to be a counterbalance, so you can breathe. With the same intent, I draped one whole side of the living room in dark-chocolate taffeta, but the opposite side—made up of French doors facing the water—has no window treatments at all. The space in between becomes simultaneously protected and wide open, directing your attention and energy outward from a sheltered vantage point.

A close cousin to timelessness is history, which very much includes the story of a home's occupants. Successfully weaving meaningful personal touches into a design also helps ensure its long-term suitability and staying power. And this family had great collections—ceramics, wood and stone sculptures, and impressive crystal specimens, among others—for us to integrate. One frequent challenge with collections is to display them with style while maintaining simplicity and focus; if you have many examples of one kind of object that you love, my advice is to group them in a limited number of nicely composed still lifes rather than scattering them on every available surface. It was a fantastic experience being able to do that so beautifully here.

Throughout the house, we kept an eye out for the essential drama of each space and employed a consistent strategy again and again. Even when the component parts of a room are different in period and detail, they speak a similar language. Nothing pushes too far in any single direction. Everything blends in a cohesive harmony.

New clients will occasionally ask, "What are people doing now?" It's not a question I'm particularly interested in. The more important issue for me is really, "What do *you* like? What's going to stand the test of time?" If you're going to make the investment of thought and care and money required to create a truly special home, surely you'll want to aim for lasting beauty, right? On this verdant bluff above the Pacific, I believe we achieved exactly that.

OPPOSITE: We played off of pleasant architectural details in the circular foyer (a sinuous iron railing and stair risers lined with patterned tile among them) by introducing a diverse range of pieces—many of them round as well, but with a chunky cubical ottoman thrown in for variety's sake.

ABOVE AND OPPOSITE: A cocoa-colored sheer reminiscent of Greek or Roman drapery separates the formal living room from an entry vestibule, where a Savonarola chair, an acrylic side table, an ancient bust, and a contemporary print speak to one another across the centuries. **OVERLEAF:** In the living room itself, chairs in assorted shapes and an armless sofa are all executed in quiet, solid ones to show the space's antiques to full advantage.

RIGHT: Certain thematic notes, such as carved statuary, crystals, and dark-colored woods, repeat again and again in various parts of the house. PAGE 25: Among the echoes of antiquity, a geometric side table and contemporary floor lamp still feel perfectly at home.

RIGHT: The dining room is very approachable, with its old refectory table and felted-wool draperies suspended by cord. I designed the console on the left to be simple and modern yet incorporate strong Old World allusions. **PAGE 28:** The owners' suite can be closed off behind a pair of ornamented doors. **PAGE 29:** In the restful, silver-gray main bedroom, an upholstered panel spans the entire wall behind the bed to embrace the nightstands.

Valance at top

Wool Sheer

Spanish Revival Chairs (in faux leather)

Custom table with drum base

knife edge

loose cushions

Waterfall skirt

the Tête Chair

PAGES 30 AND 31: An almost Parsons-like custom table with a drum base sits beneath a similarly shaped light fixture in the breakfast nook, attended by Spanish chairs and cradled in a semicircle of luminous sheers.
RIGHT: The family room exhibits the same chocolate and white palette that is prevalent throughout the house. Another way to remain timeless is to use cohesive colors.

PAGES 34, 35, AND OVERLEAF: With a view like this, what else is there to say? It's California. It's all about the year-round experience of outdoor living. Given the home's good traditional architecture and the ocean beyond, we had no reason to reinvent the wheel. Great white slipcovers were the way to go, plus a draped cabana for those occasions when a bit of shelter is needed.

Sanctuary

Bendita, meaning "blessed" in Spanish, is a word often used by the owners to describe this secluded compound, which sits within view of the Gulf of Mexico in Corpus Christi, Texas. And blessed is precisely how you feel here from the moment you drive through the arched portal that leads inside. Although located just a few minutes from downtown, the interlocked cluster of main house and multiple outbuildings—a collage of red-tiled roofs, creamy stucco walls, palms, flower beds, and grassy lawns, all stitched together by brick and stone pathways—has an atmosphere that is far removed from its near-urban surroundings, calling to mind instead the restfulness of an off-the-beaten-path coastal villa in California.

We were involved in every facet of this project, from the basics of the site plan down to the detailing of the cabinets. And perhaps the most important defining characteristic of the residence is that, despite its undeniably elegant demeanor, it does duty as a busy, multigenerational home. The spaces are occupied day in and day out by a large family, and they were designed to hold up to that kind of use while maintaining their beauty. In essence, our charge was to create a work of art that can be lived in—art that visually delights and at the same time flexes and adapts to the needs of the people inhabiting it, elevating their daily experiences.

If the home's architecture has the austerity of an early Southwestern hacienda, with its collection of simple rounded arches and the occasional ogee flourish, the interior fittings and furniture tend toward a measure of baroque exuberance that's inflected with contemporary attitude. From the custom Egyptian limestone floor I envisioned for the circular foyer to the dining room's sleek brass-and-marble table to the torch-like sconce and gilded grass cloth wallcovering adorning the powder room, each item, each detail is the result of painstaking consideration and care. Everything has a special pedigree; there's not a throwaway piece to be found.

OPPOSITE: A sketch of this home's foyer previews at a glance many of the project's main design themes: distinctive, characterful furnishings take pride of place within a more subdued architectural setting. Color is used sparingly, for emphasis, and traditional motifs frequently get a modernized or impressionistic treatment. The overall look is Mediterranean with a contemporary spin.

PAGES 40 AND 41: Unembellished plaster walls keep the tall foyer feeling relatively spare despite the drama of a handrail that I designed to swoop and swirl right down into the floor. The pierced-metal sconces, large and detailed as they may be, are only two-dimensional, and a modern stair runner, abstract-patterned floor, and open-cage Spanish chandelier all help guard against stuffiness.

PAGES 42, 43, AND OPPOSITE: The double-height living room is a meeting place for items both baroque—the massive carved-wood chandelier and a gilded gondola chair—and clean-lined: four bronze drum coffee tables and an armless sofa I designed (I especially love its bronze feet). The rug features overscale traditional motifs. ABOVE: Florid lines are toned down by the crusty patina of age.

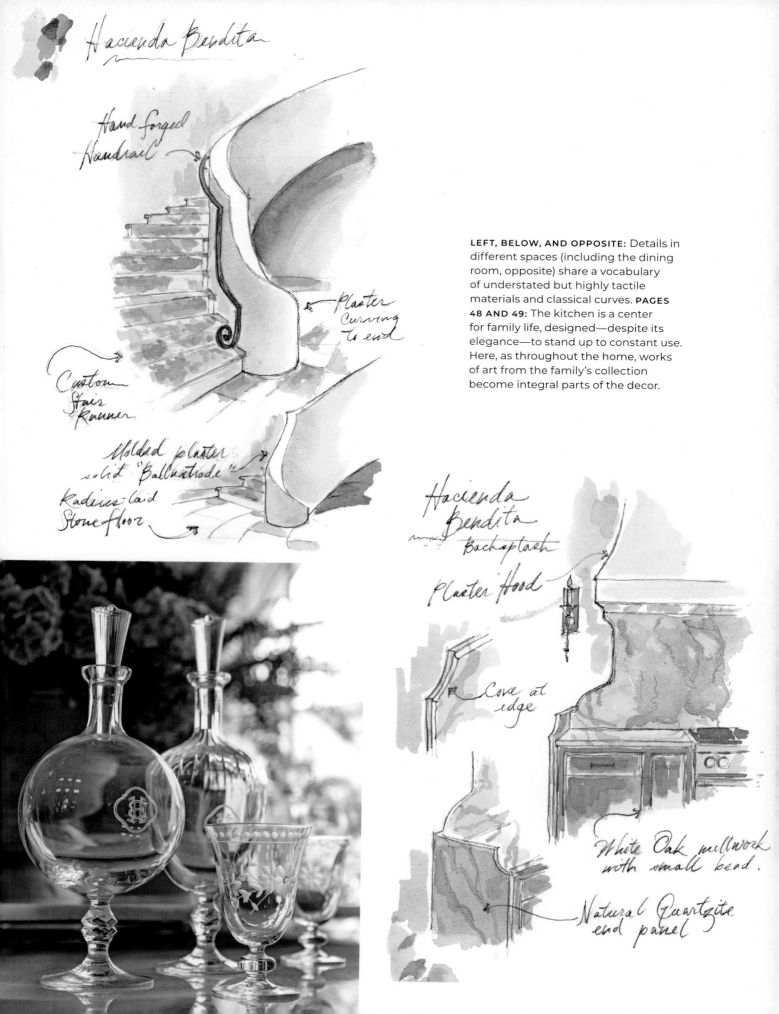

Hacienda Bendita

Hand forged
Handrail

Plaster
Curving
to end

Custom
Stair
Runner

Molded plaster
solid "Balustrade"

Radius-laid
Stone floor

LEFT, BELOW, AND OPPOSITE: Details in different spaces (including the dining room, opposite) share a vocabulary of understated but highly tactile materials and classical curves. **PAGES 48 AND 49:** The kitchen is a center for family life, designed—despite its elegance—to stand up to constant use. Here, as throughout the home, works of art from the family's collection become integral parts of the decor.

Hacienda Bendita
Backsplash

Plaster Hood

Cove at edge

White Oak millwork
with small bead.

Natural Quartzite
end panel

In many ways, we didn't hold back in terms of luxury, yet the total effect never goes over the top. Even the most imposing spaces are at the same time restrained and approachable. Ornate is played against pared-down, texture juxtaposed with smoothness, in an intentional balancing act. The family's collection of contemporary art—paintings, drawings, photography, works in neon and cardboard, many by women artists—is an especially strong counterweight to the more extravagantly decorative notes in the home.

Consistent colors and a limited (but luxe) palette of surface finishes also help reinforce an overall sense of harmony. Vanilla-hued plaster sheathes the majority of the walls, darkening to a rich charcoal in the bar and wine room. Black-and-white encaustic tiles provide some pattern in decorative niches. Accents are primarily shades of gold and bronze, including the wine room doors. Only here and there did we allow in anything brighter—a tomato red sectional in the family room, a swath of green crushed velvet on a living room chair—and one or two focal points are embellished with draped fabric.

As grand estates do, this residence includes generous entertaining spaces, where a multitude of relatives, friends, and business associates can gather, as well as wonderful private areas for the household. To name a few: a serenely sumptuous bedroom and bathroom suite for the husband and wife, which opens onto their own exclusive courtyard; stylish separate offices for both him and her; a lively lounge adjoining the kitchen, which serves as a homework space and hangout central for the younger generation; a protected outdoor dining loggia and pool pavilion; and . . . the list goes on. (There's even a family chapel.) Formal and informal, social and everyday—all aspects of life are catered to beautifully.

Despite its scale, this is a welcoming home. It doesn't overpower. We start from the calmness and structure of classical design and reinterpret it for modern living. Mediterranean references are rooted in history; Moroccan elements add a touch of the exotic. Carpets throughout the house are based on traditional motifs, but faded or abstracted—softened, almost as if being recalled in a dream.

The final impression here is one of modesty combined with magnificence. Challenging as it was to find the right proportions of each, the successful blend is what gives this amazing dwelling its tranquility and refinement, making it a blessed place apart, even amid the bustle of daily existence.

OPPOSITE: The bar has an air of North African romance with its golden fretwork screen, black plaster, and marble. An antique alabaster light fixture and concealed LEDs lend the shelf an atmospheric glow. OVERLEAF: More intense colors animate informal family spaces like this relaxed lounge. The room's sunny yellow and midnight blue speak to the *Sanctuary* art piece (see page 49) in the adjoining kitchen, and outdoor fabrics are used strategically for longevity and ease of care.

RIGHT: Sculptural furnishings, both antique and new, inhabit a calm, soft-blue cocoon in the main bedroom, which opens out to a private terrace. Gold highlights in the bed, chandelier, and Giacometti-like fire screen add a hint of sizzle.
OVERLEAF: Exquisite touches abound in the primary suite. **PAGES 58 AND 59:** With its marble mosaic floor, soaking tub, suspended plaster ceiling, nickel lanterns, and a pair of almost treelike antique candelabras, the principal bath is perhaps the most unabashedly opulent space in the house.

ABOVE: Pointed arches and an allover coating of waterproof *tadelakt* plaster in a faded aqua-mint hue transform the pool house bath into an ethereal Moroccan hammam.
OPPOSITE: An outdoor dining loggia provides a pleasantly shady spot for alfresco meals when the steamy South Texas climate permits. The mixture of furniture was chosen to be stylish and simultaneously stand up to the elements.

Taken Away

There is a moment of pure magic when you pass the beautifully carved wooden doors of this home in Austin's Tarrytown neighborhood. In that instant, you feel transported out of the city, beyond the borders of Texas, even, and off to some completely other place and time.

The street entrance opens into a paseo, a sheltered passage where a pierced-metal Moroccan lantern hangs above an antique chest and softly worn brick is laid in a simple herringbone pattern underfoot. The sound of trickling water comes through a second tall opening ahead, accompanied by a view toward the enticing light, foliage, pea gravel, and warm red roof tiles of an interior courtyard. Peacefulness and a touch of enchantment suffuse the atmosphere.

While the house was designed and built quite recently, its wonderful mingling of rhythmic shapes and rough, tactile surfaces suggests age, history, and far-flung destinations. Spanish influence is obvious—though other Mediterranean locales, like Capri or the remoter Greek islands, come equally to mind.

A complementary theme becomes evident as you linger in the central courtyard, however: notes of restraint, simplicity, and modernity. These unexpected ingredients temper the overall romance, keeping it from being too much. Glass-and-steel windows looking out from the home's living room have crisp, rectangular panes, although we painted the muntins a greenish putty color to soften their geometry. The Parsons-esque pergola supports a suspended canvas shade (the form is based on southern European models Autumn and I have noticed several times during our travels), and the central firepit we installed is an intentionally unembellished circle of carved stone. Both are elements that could seem plain on their own, but they're just right surrounded by gracious, comfortable furniture and luscious landscaping.

OPPOSITE: Where, exactly, do "outside" and "inside" begin and end? The entry I envisioned here unfolds only gradually, as visitors come in the street door, move through the covered paseo and out into a courtyard (that, although technically outdoors, is still a private, protected space), and finally step into the house proper through the steel-and-glass wall at the far side.

PAGES 64–65, 66, AND 67: Glass-and-steel windows in the living room form a decidedly contemporary backdrop to an array of comfortable furniture that includes a modern armchair covered in taupe leather and sofas clad in a combination of waxed linen (for the bodies) and an easy-care outdoor corduroy (for the cushions). Brighter color and pattern are reserved for throw pillows and the dramatic carved-wood ceiling. **OPPOSITE AND ABOVE:** Slipcovers on the dining room's tall chairs feature couture details like the lacing.

That push and pull—evocative and picturesque yet relaxed, somewhat spare, maybe even a tad edgy—represents a stylistic polarity carried through in all parts of the house. It's almost like the ebb and flow of breathing in and out—and that breath gives life here.

In the interiors, we incorporated the best of the family's Spanish and Italian antiques and combined them with similarly resonant architectural finds. A huge wooden panel on the living room ceiling is from Indonesia by way of an antiques dealer in the Texas Hill Country. A stripped set of lovely Belgian doors, which we happened upon at the Round Top Antiques Fair, lines a rear gallery through which a powder room, storage, and the couple's private spaces are accessed. Despite originating from different continents and diverse cultures, the two finds share a common textural quality that plays well in this environment. And integrating such aspects of the past adds a layer of rich nostalgia to a home.

The trick was never to let things get too heavy. We gave the leather dining chairs slipcovers of light, hand-blocked fabrics, and other decorative items were either spaced out or gathered into harmonious groups. Each weighty or intensely ornamental object is strategically set as an anchor, and the contemporary pieces and custom creations serve as counterpoints.

A calculated balance between pale and dark colors (a lot of white, just enough of a deep graphite) boosts the level of drama in these rooms as well. Lighting fixtures, in particular, are highly graphic, like the strokes in a charcoal or pencil drawing. Their repeated curves and diagonals function as a unifying device at the same time as they provide vivid contrast. Only in the main bedroom do shady hues get the upper hand, for a look that's both snug and undeniably sexy.

At the front of the home is the casita, a small, connected guesthouse that screens the courtyard from the street. If the main house borrows some of the qualities of an Aegean villa, here you've now sailed out to a little fishing cottage. Everything inside is simplified, more rustic or casual, and contrasts are heightened.

The magic of this place, in the end, comes from the dances between old and new, light and dark, found and fabricated. It's approachable and clear, but with a consistent rhythm of dynamic gesture. It's not a huge home, but it makes an oversize impression because moving through it is such an adventure. It surprises you, continually revealing itself as you spend time there. In the middle of Austin, you exist in another realm: one of freedom, calmness, and restoration, where you can exhale and then be filled up again.

PRECEDING SPREAD: Varying surface qualities—from smooth and polished to abraded and rough—enliven each room. OPPOSITE: We didn't want the kitchen to feel too much like a kitchen, which is why there are no upper cabinets and the vent hood is hidden within a decorative niche that includes a marble shelf for the display of art and objects. PAGES 74 AND 75: Two options were considered for the breakfast nook, one including a sofa and oval table; in the end, the clients opted for a full, U-shaped banquette. The perky mustard-colored ottoman is one of our custom designs.

Floor
Lamps →

Sofa with
outdoor fabric →

Stone end
table →

Custom pedestal
table

← Curtain
(Butler's
Pantry
beyond)

Leather arm
chairs

Breakfast Nook
Option 1

Banquette in
outdoor fabric →

Wall lime →

← Curtain
(Butler's
Pantry
beyond)

Antique pull-up
chairs

Custom
table w/ iron
base

Breakfast Nook
Option 2

RIGHT: Every detail in the house was carefully chosen for maximum visual and tactile effect, from the antique hand-forged latch on the powder room door to a pair of salvaged architectural details displayed on a chest in the couple's bedroom.

RIGHT: The dark-hued walls of the principal bedroom read black at first glance, but in fact have wonderful undertones of blue, green, and brown that shift as the light changes throughout the day. OVERLEAF: The casita is the only part of the house that looks out directly to the street, and, although still elegant, it has a more casual mood, with slipcovered furniture arranged around a coffee table that was sliced from a weathered tree trunk.

ABOVE, BELOW, OPPOSITE AND OVERLEAF:
Both the casita and the main home's living
room have access to the central courtyard,
which is set up for outdoor living and dining.
We added a trough-like fountain to make it
as pleasant to the ear as it is to the eye.

New Life

There was once a project I carried very close to my heart because of the time, energy, and effort that had been poured into it. The whole process of creation had been intense as well as immensely rewarding; the outcome was a home I was extremely proud of. So, years later, when I heard that the home was to be sold, I mentally closed that chapter of my career and filed the experience away as a favorite memory. I let it go. Then a funny thing happened: not long after, new clients called us to make over a house they had just bought . . . and it was *that* house. An exciting beginning for them was, for me, a project that had come back to life.

The residence is laid out along a ridge overlooking Barton Creek in Austin, its main rooms lined up to capture the view across the back, where the land drops off dramatically and Texas starts to grow more rugged. The architecture has deep southern European roots. We mixed in a dash of Spanish influence, a lot of Tuscan feeling, and a bit of the South of France. Plans were originally developed hand in hand with the architect in the kind of collaboration we love to be part of, whenever possible, so that floor plans, materials, and furnishings all evolve together. Quite a few of the interior details were conceived on-site during construction, in partnership with the artisans who would be executing the work. In that sense, the home was built as it would have been hundreds of years ago.

Authenticity was a watchword from day one. The main house's stonework rests in traditional deep-set mortar. At the edge of the roof, a period- and geography-appropriate *génoise* detail appears beneath the eaves: rows of inset barrel tiles receding gradually into the wall surface. The plaster indoors isn't waxed to a mirror gloss, but instead has a matte finish that's gentle to the touch as well as to the eye. The walls, like many of the home's textures, embrace you with softness and warmth—with a loving, life-filled quality, if you will.

With such an eloquent architectural setting already in place, the redesign became a matter of lightening the home's interiors and making them a little more casual. We employed more whites and a lot of pale icy blues in this version, whereas the original vibe was more mysterious. That's also why I threw in so many

OPPOSITE: Romance and restraint are two important qualities I aim for in my interiors, and that's not as contradictory as it may sound. Romance evokes an emotional connection; restraint keeps the effect from shading over into kitsch or caricature. In this Tuscan-feeling living room sketch, custom "opera cloak" chairs I designed definitely lean toward the flamboyant, while a little contemporary side table helps rein them in.

ABOVE AND OPPOSITE: Mixing and matching objects is an art form, and a special pleasure comes from throwing together items that are unexpected. In this group, a sleek glass lamp rubs shoulders with a vase that might just have been dug up out of the earth. **PAGES 90 AND 91:** Interior sheers frame the living room as seen from this home's foyer, and a rhyming set of white curtains frames a view out toward the Texas hills.

Stone floor

Dining Rm →

Gathered draping at front

Knife-edge back cushion

Overall slip-covered effect

Gathered at back?

Slight break

The Opera Cloak

THIS SPREAD AND OVERLEAF: Because the living room's boundaries are symmetrical, but the function of the room is not, a traditional mirrored arrangement wouldn't work. So, the furniture plan that evolved is organized along an axis from the home's front door to the back window, but it also accommodates a fireplace in one corner and access to the rear terrace in another. Discreet pink accents are drawn from the tonality of a favorite painting of the clients', and a few touches of dark wood help anchor the otherwise light-toned space.

RIGHT: In the library, automotive paint gives the shelves their shine, with the inset niches upholstered for variety of texture. We picked up the old rose color from the contemporary portrait hanging above the sofa, and I added a slight flare to the club chair arms to rhyme with the wonderfully angular white onyx lamp. **PAGES 98 AND 99:** Louis XVI chairs (in an Italian version) are joined by a curved banquette with simple channel upholstery in the dining room, just to keep things cozy. The abstract rug provides plenty of interest underfoot.

slipcovers: they're practical, fresh, and used all the time in Italy—particularly in country and coastal houses. Beautiful swaths of linen can make a room sing and help its other contents shine that much more.

The living room is stunning, with its outer envelope of rugged stone encircling all the white upholstery. Then, in the middle, we're back to blond-colored stone again with a hand-carved table from Formations accompanied by three custom ottomans. A tall chair clad in white cowhide stands regally nearby, along with a pair of oh-so-romantic "opera cloak" armchairs I devised—all beneath a platinum-painted papier-mâché chandelier made in Mexico. Scattered hints of dark wood—an antique secretary, a tiny European side table— peek out here and there to provide just enough weight and balance.

The home's central core, the area around the entry and living room, is the most traditional, with the atmosphere becoming more contemporary as you head out to the spaces at either end. Our idea was for the house to feel like a historic structure that had been graciously renovated, and the more functional parts, used for eating, sleeping, and bathing, are the ones that would most have needed updating. The change in tone shows dramatically in the kitchen, where walls, soffits, and ceiling are covered in pale, ruler-straight parallel planking. We put white lacquer on the formerly espresso-stained cabinets, added natural quartzite countertops, and changed out the chandelier with a geometric-botanical fantasy in white plaster.

Similarly gorgeous outdoor spaces step down along one side and in the rear of the house. A small patio for outdoor dining sits beneath a hand-forged iron canopy. Cascades of limestone steps meander toward an assembly of pergola, firepit, and fountain surrounding a tidy lawn and pool. The cabana, built of dry-stacked stone and meant to resemble a repurposed gardener's shed, contains a kitchen, living room, and expansive porch, all spread out beneath reclaimed beams that had a diluted white stain put on to give them an even more aged appearance.

I love that this house has held up so well over the years and has been able to accommodate two quite disparate, yet equally beguiling, design visions. In its present form, the home remains genuine in its allusions to history while incorporating notes of modern restraint. We wanted to preserve what was already wonderful about the place and at the same time make it unique and special for its current residents—a challenge, I'd say, that feels something like a resurrection.

OPPOSITE: The reworked kitchen has a modern vibe, despite a Versailles-pattern stone floor that hints at age. The stainless-steel hood and backsplash I originally did for the home's previous owners still look great in the updated scheme. PAGES 102 AND 103: The breakfast area is light not just in color but also in mood, with a crisp, white banquette and slightly odd old klismos chairs surrounding a vintage Eero Saarinen pedestal table. PAGES 104–105: The Mediterranean spirit can be found everywhere. PAGES 106–107: I don't like throwaway spaces, so it was important to do something interesting in this pass-through adjoining the dining room. We found these architectural fragments on 1stDibs, and I designed the low-back benches to go under them.

ABOVE: Visual anchors come in many forms. **OPPOSITE:** The serene color scheme for the principal bedroom was inspired by a fur-like rug the couple already owned that drifts somewhere between silver and charcoal. And, again, you'll see a play of old against new, as with the chandelier and the two standing lamps in the window. **OVERLEAF:** The pool area is framed by a cabana and a pergola constructed with reclaimed timbers.

Belonging

Many of my homes take their owners on a journey, and this beach house in Galveston, Texas, is no exception. The journey in this case, however, has more to do with time and the emotional resonances of the past than with geography.

Standing near the eastern point of the island, the house looks south toward the Gulf of Mexico, where, at night, you can see the lights of ships lined up in the channel, waiting their turn to head into the Port of Houston. It's an entrancing prospect, like your own personal Christmas display year-round. The neighborhood is largely populated by grand, white-painted Greek Revival homes, their already-lofty silhouettes raised even higher to avoid coastal flooding. Standing cheek by jowl, they make an impressive rampart on both sides of the street.

But then, as you continue down the block, a putty-colored building comes into view that's a bit lower, noticeably simpler, and more unassuming. An indefinable air about it suggests deep roots and the mellowness of age. Is it an old warehouse that once served the local "Mosquito Fleet" of shrimp boats, now converted as living quarters? Or maybe a leftover cottage, the sole remaining vestige of a fishing camp that formerly stood on the site? Surely there's a backstory here, the kind of lingering connection to bygone days that can enrich our experience of the present.

That's the atmosphere we aimed for in creating this brand-new home, and what, I think, accounts for its unquestionable appeal. Because it doesn't push: it takes time to reveal itself architecturally, and the interiors share the same easygoing, enfolding quality—exactly what you need when you're relaxing at the beach, right?

The home's entry, behind a cheerful, red-painted door, is on the ground level. Visitors are greeted by the knotty tangle of a cypress-root console and a selection of crustacean-themed art in the foyer—an immediate indication that we're not trying to be too serious. The tall, open main living and dining areas, plus the kitchen,

OPPOSITE: Second homes are places where you can be a little more lighthearted, a little more adventurous, than you might wish to be in a primary home. This upstairs porch at a Galveston beach house is an extension of the living room and expresses exactly what the home is about: relaxation, recharging, and perhaps a bit of nostalgia for "the good old days."

ABOVE AND OPPOSITE: A compact ground-level foyer gives little hint of the height and lightness that exist in the home's upstairs main floor, where posts and beams outline a rhythmic structure that the interior furnishings exist within. A steel dining table and diagonal braces attached to the columns tie in with the notion that this was once a warehouse.

are upstairs; they have great proportions. Then the top level is special because it's tucked under the roof and there are all these sloped ceilings. It reminds me of blanket forts I built when I was a kid, making the family's private spaces feel like spots where you can sneak away.

In order to further the illusion that antique construction had been modernized, we worked hard with the builder and their artisans to give the trim, beams, and columns on the main floor a weathered appearance. Having *everything* seem aged would be oppressive and too much, so windows, doors, and ceilings are painted flat (the ceilings in a pale blue gray). The effect is one of an old timber frame that has been filled in with more recent materials.

Furniture in the house is a combination of cozy, comfy upholstery and sturdy, textured pieces meant to relate to the ruggedness of the architecture—*faux bois* side tables or ones of cast metal that look almost as if they're encrusted with shells or coral or barnacles, for example, or consoles apparently fashioned out of old crates. Meals are served on an industrial steel table that had to be craned in through the French doors on the second level, and the main bedroom includes a battered metal cart once used to transport mail in a post office. Light fixtures lean toward the old-fashioned and industrial, while window treatments are deliberately minimal—woven shades, primarily, and only an occasional pair of draperies.

I put more pattern into these spaces than I usually do. Differing configurations of parallel stripes and plaids in nearly every room, as well as a scattering of *X* shapes, echo the home's exposed structural members and the angled iron tie rods that brace the tops of columns. Muted colors keep the combined result under control: blacks and whites, beiges, a few soft blue greens and blue grays, most giving the impression that they've been a little faded by the sun. We employed textiles and rugs that seem like they could be old, even if they have a twist to add some edge to an otherwise vintage-y interior.

The lesson of this seaside haven, I'd say, is how powerful it can be when what you do on the inside with your finishes and your furnishings tells the same story the house itself is telling. There are occasions when you can create a contrast, of course, but you still want to draw connection points. There's one overall idea. We intended to evoke emotion and a sense of nostalgia here, despite the fact that the home was built from scratch. Instead of specific memories, it conjures the *idea* of memory, of lived history and belonging. And it doesn't try to be more than it is, which is what makes it so very, very comfortable.

OPPOSITE: The kitchen's backsplash tile and bead-board-lined cabinets also play into the home's "industrial" backstory. An old-fashioned light fixture with conical milk-glass shades feels like it could have come from a 1920s bookkeeper's office. **OVERLEAF:** The eminently inviting living room looks south toward the Gulf of Mexico. Intermingled with the comfy upholstery, a few chunky wood pieces relate to the ruggedness of the home's architecture.

ABOVE AND OPPOSITE: Much of the home's color scheme is monochromatic, with light and dark neutrals playing the biggest role. Patterns (with some exceptions, naturally!) lean toward the linear: various stripes and plaids. Slipcovers are employed for cleanability as well as for their distinctly casual vibe. The few nautical allusions we allowed, such as the buoy light next to the family room sofa, have a tongue-in-cheek quality.

RIGHT: Soft blues and celadons predominate in the primary bedroom, where a plain iron bed and other furnishings appear to have been simply accumulated over time. Rugs and textiles seem as if they could be old as well, even when they represent a more modern take on tradition.

ABOVE AND OPPOSITE: The ground-level entertaining deck hits a more exuberant note, with its playful hanging swing and teal Moroccan rug. Still, the look is only a slightly amped-up version of what you see indoors. Inside or out, nothing about this house assaults your senses or tries too hard. It just sits down beside you and says, "Hey, what's up?"

Imparting Identity

Whether I'm designing for a new house or decorating an existing one, the first challenge is to discover what the home's identity ought to be. Identity isn't necessarily inherent in a dwelling, even when there's already great architecture in place. An identity must be imagined and crafted, imparted through design decisions and their execution. The decoration helps give a final shape to a home's identity, determining how the home functions and feels. And whether I'm decorating for myself or for clients, I want a residence to be completely infused with a sense of who its owners are at their best.

This home in Fort Worth was unquestionably grand, with beautiful features—and because of its size could easily have come across as too formal. Our task was to make it simultaneously as welcoming and approachable as the couple who would be living there, while still embracing its classical attitude. The rooms needed to be supplied with moments of human scale, a little edge, and a good deal of warmth that would draw visitors in and enfold them. One of my favorite strategies for achieving this kind of effect is to break the rules slightly, to go a shade against the grain.

I'll give you an example: the living room is big, which is great for hosting large social events but called for finesse when it came to deciding on a layout. Architecturally, the space is oriented symmetrically around a fireplace; therefore, in general, you would anticipate a similarly symmetrical arrangement for the furniture— which I didn't completely shy away from. Rather than have the arrangement facing the fireplace, however, I turned the whole thing around so that it's centered on how people enter the room and broke it up into two seating groups pushed toward the ends of the space and anchored in the middle by an old, rustic English table we found on 1stDibs.

Although the mirrored groupings each share the same *L*-shaped configuration of two sofas (a pairing of one from Dennis & Leen and another custom-designed by us), they're varied with different chairs and occasional tables so that nothing is too predictable. Set up this way, the room entices people in and provides plenty of space for them to interact and flow easily from one conversation to the next.

OPPOSITE: Subtly diverse harmonies define the experience of this Fort Worth house. A custom console and bronze floor lamps that are a somewhat modern take on Empire style, which speak to the curtain rod and steel windows in the dining room. Beautiful ombré draperies were inherited from the home's previous owners—you shouldn't feel obligated to change elements of a room that already work well.

PRECEDING SPREAD: The main living room is meant for large social functions, which the owners host frequently. **THIS SPREAD:** A symmetrical overall furniture plan is varied with occasional nonmatching pieces. Easily movable seating is one secret to making a room work for a crowd, so a cluster of small, linen-covered stools is tucked around the center table, ready to be pulled over wherever they are needed.

OPPOSITE: A vellum-covered Parsons console in the living room adds a little bit of a Jean-Michel Frank vibe, without going too far in that direction. Antique Chinese figures and a large gilded-wood finial already belonged to the couple. I love pulling together dissimilar objects to make a persuasive composition. **ABOVE:** The elaborate vase by Shari Mendelson on the living room's central table is made—believe it or not—entirely out of recycled plastic water bottles.

The nearby library could have been organized around a desk, as a conventional office. Instead, we took a mid-century Italian bronze-top table and ran it perpendicular to the window, where it can be used as a partners desk, or the room—with its dark-painted walls, stripped-wood chandelier, and shelves full of antique books and stone-colored pottery—can also now double as an intimately romantic spot for private dining, reading, or watching TV. What might otherwise have been a workaday space—or even not used—is now a lovely, multifunctional lounge, and keeps calling you back over and over.

We layered differing styles of furniture in this house, including occasional combinations that are intentionally a bit "wrong." For the dining room, I designed rolling, leather-upholstered chairs to rub shoulders with the couple's existing side chairs and kept their round table—not typical practice in a rectangular setting. We changed out the stair railing in the home's foyer for a simple one that has a touch of art deco to it, then paired it with huge, almost medieval-looking iron sconces. Throw in an old French country chandelier and you are definitely crossing boundaries. Done carefully, this practice will keep spaces feeling personally "collected" rather than perfectly put together.

The same story holds true for materials: I'll bounce back and forth between metal, wood, leather, and luscious rugs and upholstery fabrics, so they're not all right next to each other and they break each other up. In a house like this one, items such as the living room's rough center table (which looks as if it could have come from an estate sale) and the same room's unassuming wooden mantel introduce a note of humility that's not quite expected. Meanwhile, the nearby vellum console adds a smidgen of sexiness to the space. Far from being too impressed with itself, the home exudes an identity that is easygoing and hospitable.

In many houses, I want the architecture, the interior details, and the furnishings to all speak the same language. Here, we mixed it up, using elements that are both old and new, more sophisticated versus more down-to-earth. Of course, stylistic flexibility doesn't mean going crazy and picking completely random things—there has to be some sort of connection, some sort of consistency. But we were judicious in our selections, and the results speak for themselves. The home continues to be grand and elegant . . . plus warm, sometimes unexpected, maybe even a touch unruly—very much like its inhabitants.

OPPOSITE: In the library, a precisely placed table can serve either as a workspace or as the ideal site for a quiet supper à deux. **OVERLEAF:** Far from being stiff or stuffy, the library contains furniture of several differing styles—from a Southeast Asian bronze drum table to a modernist leather lamp that resembles a giant sugar cube—all set atop an abstract botanical rug.

Easel with Aot Light

Platinum Gilded Table

Bleached wood bench

LEFT AND CENTER: A little grouping of stools, an hourglass-shaped table, flowers, and an easel-mounted painting lends graciousness to a gallery that runs between the home's foyer and dining room, without impeding traffic or interfering with the view of the courtyard outside.

BELOW: In a comparable arrangement for the principal bedroom, a reading chair and chaise longue flank a table that's only twenty-six inches high for relaxed access to morning coffee or a laptop.
OPPOSITE: A glimpse of the dining room beckons in the distance.

Reupholstered Lounge Chair

Heavy Linen Draperies

26" High Table for Coffee

Custom Chaise

Main Bedroom Sitting

Area Rug Over Carpet

RIGHT: The "candles" in the dining room's Italian chandelier are long crystal shafts, lit with LEDs, that glow from base to tip. An unexpectedly tiny gilt mirror and equally diminutive painting create piquant accents in an otherwise large-scale room.
OVERLEAF: The family room is more contemporary than the rest of the house, with its swoop-backed custom sofa and smooth gray upholstery fabrics. Still, an eclectic mood predominates, given the African ladder placed in the back corner and the odd little faux-deer-leg table in the foreground.

RIGHT: The couple's bed is new, but it feels like an antique and—even without draping—its canopy helps break up the expansive space into more intimate "interiors within an interior." The wonderfully (and literally) florid bedside lamps are vintage Italian and make an enlivening counterpoint to the understated aspects of the room. The figured rug layered over plain carpet performs a similar function.

A Sheltered Place

Situated on the margin of a beautiful greenbelt on Austin's west side, this house was made to be a serene, secluded oasis. Like homes in many parts of Europe and Mexico, it's cloistered behind a wall on the street side for privacy and looks out instead onto a hidden courtyard along one edge of the property. The home has the feel of a little villa or estate on the outskirts of Florence—not quite formal enough for the center of town, but (despite thick, angled window embrasures and roughly surfaced stone walls) not too countryish, either.

You come into the dwelling gradually, via a progression of spaces. The courtyard's antique gates are perpendicular to the inner front door, so when they open you're initially greeted by a tableau of artistically enclosed nature—gravel, plants in stone pots, overhanging live oaks, a fanciful oversize lantern—rather than seeing straight through to the interior.

Inside the court, a steel-and-glass entrance on the right leads to a small stone foyer. There's nothing as staid as a console here, just an old wooden bench holding a gathering of decorative objects, like a casual meeting of friends, and an abstract painting hung low enough to become part of the composition. One more threshold, framed with heavy, dark velvet draperies, finally gives access to the living room. The whole sequence is one of revealed layers, a theatrical entry that concludes as the rear of the house opens up to a vista of undulating hills, a craggy cliff, and the sweeping creek valley below.

The monochromatic interiors of this quiet retreat are moody and elegant, enveloping their occupants in a cocoon of sophisticated European calm. Drama and contrast come from variations in tone, not color, with deep shades adding weight. What really sets the house apart, though, is its palette of materials. Four components combine to create a consistent—and compelling—balance of variety versus sameness throughout.

OPPOSITE: The delicate lines of a John Saladino iron coffee table and a carved Renaissance stool seem as if they are dancing amid a muted sea of limestone, velvet, and cowhide. Such moments of low-key drama—enough to contribute vitality but never too emphatic—tell the story of this home.

OPPOSITE AND ABOVE: At first it might seem that there are too many things in the entry foyer. Yet the abundance and variousness of them all add up to a warm welcome.
OVERLEAF: Without a lot of color in play, energy comes from differences in shape, tone, texture, and material. In the living room, that spectrum extends from the bare simplicity of a pair of modern lampshades to the intricate complexities of a gilded mirror.

RIGHT: Small design moments throughout the home are variations on a consistent theme. As in a piece of music, several motives will combine into a harmonious background against which a divergent strand of melody stands out in relief.

First, you have limestone, which is the most pervasive design element in the whole house; there's a lot of it in both walls and floors, and it's a powerful presence. Then there's wood: we included at least some amount of stained wood in nearly every space. There's also metal in each room, whether an iron chandelier, a nickel cabinet pull, or a custom steel breakfast table. Finally, there are intentionally eye-catching items that energize the subtler harmonies around them. Using those extra, unexpected ingredients—like throwing a jalapeño pepper into a margarita—is what makes the home really come alive.

In the living room, a pair of wonderfully ornate gilded candlesticks, silk damask pillows, a Renaissance revival tapestry, and a sinuous blue-gray pattern hand-painted onto the skirt of a velvet armchair, among other things, help add the necessary intensity, standing out against the more restrained profiles of the other furniture in the space. Swoopy arms and a thicket of dangling wooden tassels on the dining room's overscale chandelier serve the same purpose, while the fixture simultaneously brings down the ceiling height for a protected feeling—akin to being under a draped canopy or beneath the branches of a tree.

In each case, the gutsy choices play their part, but they don't come off as overly extravagant since they are embedded in a background web of related textures and colors and repeated geometries. The painted shapes on the living room chair skirt, for example, echo the curved ends of the daybed next to them, and that daybed and a facing sofa are both upholstered in an identical combination of leather and faux fur. When you start with a strong, cohesive scheme, you shouldn't shy away from putting in a few showy flourishes, because you might get magic at the end.

Ultimately, the strength and solidity of the home's stone walls, an interplay of highly tactile materials, and an intimate, human scale came together to produce the haven we envisioned for our clients. Full of nods to Old World luxury, this is a residence that embraces its occupants, almost like the wing of an eagle safeguarding its young in the nest.

OPPOSITE: A low coffee table and chairs add unassuming appeal to the courtyard, providing visual respite from the busyness and movement of the environment. PAGES 156 AND 157: Stone yields to smooth plaster when you reach the urbane dining room. Certain decorative elements, such as the chandelier, scalloped sofa back, and huge tassels, are almost too much—but in a good way. PAGES 158–159: Three blue pillows make the walnut-paneled library the most "colorful" space in the house. Instead of a stone room with wood furniture in it, here we have a wood room with stone accents.

ABOVE AND OPPOSITE: The powder room pairs a custom marble vanity with a Fortuny pendant lamp. We found the magnificent door in Mexico and had it resized by an Austin craftsman. **PAGES 162 AND 163:** Mornings can be spent immersed in the spectacular hillside view from the breakfast room. I designed the steel table with a top that's ultrathin to contrast with the weighty base and surrounding upholstery. **PAGES 164–165:** In Austin's climate, this rear terrace is usable nearly year-round, with the fireplace lit for comfort on nippy days.

Good to Great

When clients approach us about working on a home they've just purchased, I am full of expectation—something like the way I imagine a novelist must feel when facing a blank page at the start of a new book. In our case, of course, the page isn't exactly blank—our design will be shaped in part by the architecture and materials already in place—but I still get a welcome glow of anticipation and enthusiasm for what we'll be able to add. In fact, the rewards of a project like this may be all the greater *because* it comes with constraints, requiring that we pour in that extra measure of imagination and ingenuity.

A perfect illustration is this house, which was purchased to serve as a getaway for a family that lives full-time out on their ranch. (That's the inverse of how things usually work in Texas: the majority of people live in the city, and the ranch house is a weekends-and-holidays destination.) When we first saw the home, it had decent bones, some quite nice finishes, loads of space, plenty of light—all good stuff. What it lacked was impact and the distinctive touches that would make stays there genuinely memorable. Given the owners' youthfulness and strong interest in Latin American culture, we decided to capture the atmosphere of a modern Central or South American resort—think Los Cabos, Riviera Maya, or one of the destinations along Mexico's Pacific coast—for their in-town escape.

A rich experience now begins at the front door, in a square foyer with hazy sheers masking all four walls. Many houses today are so open that they lose any sense of definition. Older houses had specific rooms for a reason: if you have no boundaries at all, you can end up feeling lost. Our mission here was to tame the home's expanses into a series of relatively intimate destinations that allow occupants a moment of containment and protection, of knowing where they are, before they are enticed onward toward a different goal—maybe only partially visible—that beckons in the distance. Moving through the house has become a journey of revelation and discovery.

Interior drapery continues its duties in the central living area, helping screen a circulation corridor away from the paired seating groups placed behind it (as well as providing privacy cover for the front and rear window walls). I use sheers in many of my projects but hung more of them in this house than anywhere else so far. They provide such softness, simultaneously outlining and blurring edges much as watercolors do.

OPPOSITE: Not showing everything all at once is critical when dealing with an open-concept home. I placed sheers to frame the doors and windows on all sides of this foyer, plus an antique rug and a strong central grouping of a trestle table with art atop it, an ottoman, and paired standing lamps to greet visitors with a space that's a destination as well as an introduction to other rooms beyond.

PRECEDING SPREAD AND THIS SPREAD: Hefty shapes and striking profiles help define a large house. The custom sofa in front of the living room window is some ten feet long, and the crushed-metal tables in front of it make an unmissable statement (as do the marvelous Italian plaster lamps, which look like clusters of massive grapes). We designed the round marble coffee table that anchors a second seating arrangement with the same idea in mind. On the color front, just enough earthy red accents, in the form of pillows and a leather armchair, pop amid the general lightness.

Many recent homes also lump together cooking, dining, and entertaining spaces as a single unit. Unless handled carefully, the arrangement can call to mind a giant apartment for me—not in a good way. So, again, we were determined in this house to separate the three functions visually, even if they do, in fact, occupy a single volume. The kitchen is signposted by two almost industrial-looking display towers that we attached to the outer corners of the island, while a long sofa with a tall back partitions off the dining area. On the opposite side of the table, three delightful little barrel chairs keep their backs turned to the living area but can easily be rolled over into it for additional seating. Divide and conquer—without actual walls.

In keeping with our vacation-resort vision, the house includes an abundance of contemporary yet relaxed furnishings. Although new things are invariably counterpointed by antiques, in this instance, even the antiques are edited and austere enough to share a modern attitude. In a simple setting, you'll often want to be a bit bolder with your decorating gestures. We put big shapes and strong geometry in a lot of places and made sure that understated furniture profiles were always elevated by some kind of plush texture, be it leather or bouclé or African beading.

When weaving a complicated pattern, it's also best to have unifying themes that run through. The many individualized spaces we worked so hard to carve out share a common color palette of assorted grays and an orangey pinky red, inspired by the beautiful herringbone brick that is spread across the home's outdoor terraces. In most rooms, the earthy or charcoal-ish colors exist as lively accents to a neutral background. Yet here and there the more assertive tones, either warm or cool, take center stage.

The art in the house, too—from an abstract canvas by a Uruguayan modernist master to an icon I commissioned from a painter on the Greek island of Santorini—plays a significant part in consolidating the home's story. I'm not enthusiastic about works of art that are chosen simply to match a room's decor, but both interior design and art *should* express complementary aspects of the owners' personalities.

Redoing a residence that already has its strong points is, for me, much like taking a basic wardrobe and investing it with some serious fashion flair. The smart method is not to try to change everything wholesale. Instead, identify and keep what already functions well, then spice it up using a limited handful of dramatic moves. Our personality-enhancing tool kit for this project consisted primarily of sheers, an engaging interplay between history and modernity, gutsy texture, and consistent color combinations. And there's nothing so-so or anonymous about this former spec house any longer.

OPPOSITE: Next to the dining room, an altar-like plaster-covered console incorporates a little circular table that could perhaps be the place to light a sacred flame. The religious aura is enhanced by a Greek icon painting I had made on Santorini for the clients and installed on a custom easel. Are these items ancient or modern? I love that there's no immediate way to tell.

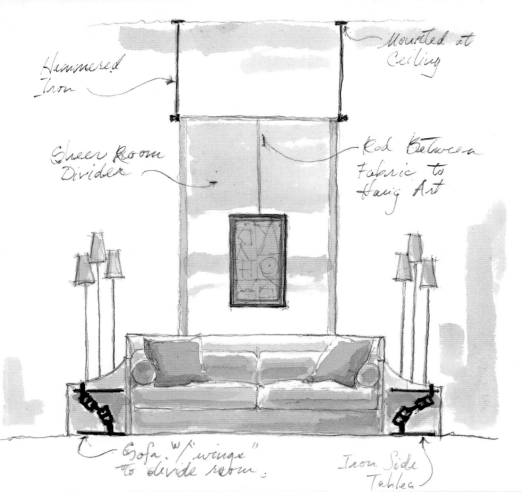

Hammered
Iron

Mounted at
Ceiling

Sheer Room
Divider

Rod Between
Fabric to
Hang Art

Sofa "wings"
to divide room.

Iron Side
Tables

LEFT AND BELOW: A suspended fabric divider cordons off the living room from a neighboring circulation space and gives it a sense of separation. I like to drop art into unusual spots: here, the abstract painting gains visual weight from being double-framed—once by its actual frame and again by the sheer panel it hangs against.

ABOVE AND RIGHT: I designed a daybed for the primary bedroom with gilded-steel ends and base and leather cushions. As a space within a space, the sitting area has real presence: the chair, with its swoop, sways to the left, and the table sways to the right. It's vibrant.

RIGHT: A pair of stainless-steel étagères marks the division between the kitchen and dining area. Brackets hold up shelving, perfect for bottled oils, baskets, potted herbs, or what have you, making the towers practical as well as decorative. A mix of different seating types, including a pair of French bistro chairs, keeps things casual and fun. **OVERLEAF:** Works of art and sculptural objects frequently play a leading role.

RIGHT: We used a bronzy embossed wallpaper to bring character to the principal bedroom, and combined a very traditional Spanish bed with contemporary chairs, lamps, and nightstands.
OVERLEAF: The draperies on the back patio have a subtle terra-cotta stripe, and upholstered furniture is interspersed with wovens for a touch of the tropical. The "bean" coffee table once again reminds us that it's the twenty-first century.

Leap of Faith

There is a side to design that's almost a form of soothsaying or predicting the future. Designers have to be able to visualize states of affairs that don't yet exist, to imagine how a house can look and function differently from the way it currently does. And clients must be prepared to trust that their designer's vision is appropriate, achievable, and will result in surroundings that are a delight to inhabit. If both parties invest fully in the partnership, the results can be magical.

When I first got to know this house in Westlake, on Austin's west side, it became clear that the element of trust would be particularly important to the process of helping it become, as the saying goes, its best self. Because if the biggest problem to be solved was pretty straightforward, it was also pretty major: the home was full of spaces that didn't work for how its owners—or any contemporary family—would want to live.

The house had been built several decades before, when the need for separate formal living and dining rooms was rarely questioned. Those "required" spaces were sited at the front of the structure, separated from the areas where people would in fact spend most of their days (such as the kitchen and family room) by a long, transverse gallery and two changes of elevation, each including a short set of stairs. At the same time, a similar high-ceilinged gallery or sunroom in the rear—stretching the entire length of the house and lined with tall, arched windows looking out over the backyard—was languishing, seldom used and practically empty.

One of the home's most appealing qualities is the way it flows in stages down a hillside, eventually opening out in the midst of several terraces and a gorgeous landscape. Consequently, I knew that the connection between the kitchen and the family room and the outdoors provided the center of gravity around which members of the household would circle.

Just because a room has a certain label on a plan doesn't mean that you have to use it for the stated purpose; you're under no legal obligation to actually put your dining table in the "dining room." Seeing

OPPOSITE: The duty of an entry is to help you make your way into and out of a home, of course, but also to provide a foretaste of what the home is meant to be. In this setting, the marriage of a rather worn leather bench, Moroccan carpet, petite octagonal table, and potted greenery immediately calls to mind the lobby of a picturesquely scruffy Latin American hotel.

185

ABOVE AND OPPOSITE: The archangel Michael presides over the front gallery, which perfectly embodies this home's engagingly retro Spanish character with its hexagonal tiles, barrel vault, and shell-capped plaster niches. **OVERLEAF:** For the living room, we created the leather screen at left to cover the television when it's not in use. The gathered furniture choices give an impression of having found their way in, piece by piece, over many decades.

another way to proceed, I flipped the whole house's scheme back to front, moving group-oriented social functions toward the rear and allotting the relatively isolated former living and dining areas to activities that genuinely benefit from some seclusion. One space is now the children's playroom, which can be shut off behind glass doors to tone down noise; the other has been turned into the mother's private retreat, a haven for her to read, rest, and recharge.

Today, the family dining table sits in the back gallery, which has been recast as a marvelous greenhouse, with masses of plants both hanging and in pots on the floor. That once-forlorn bit of real estate also accommodates a lounging area and a nook for more intimate or informal meals, serving overall as an inviting botanical segue from indoor living to exterior nature and vice versa.

Although the house had other oddities that required fixing—we ended up redoing half of the kitchen for better usability, shifted the orientation of a powder room that previously opened into that kitchen, and converted an office you inexplicably had to walk through to get to the main bedroom into a more appropriate library and TV room—our intent wasn't to change everything simply for the sake of change. Certain details with noteworthy character—a barrel-vaulted ceiling, plaster wall niches, floors of hexagonal terra-cotta tile—cried out to be kept, and even led us to a romantic conception of the place as exotic, tropical, and slightly dilapidated: a villa outside of Havana, perhaps, or an old-fashioned hotel somewhere in Central America.

The rest was a matter of layering in a selection of wonderfully patinated and textured furnishings. Nothing is too precious; you'll see a lot of crustiness and broken pieces, the artwork has an earthy feel to it, and many of the rugs are Moroccan: faded, nubby, loosely woven. Light fixtures also received a lot of attention throughout; you give a simple room a glamorous piece of jewelry and it goes a million miles. The whole mix comes together in glorious imperfection.

In rethinking this house, we stepped back and ignored preconceived ideas about "proper" layout and room use. Addressing its challenges demanded flexibility—and faith that an uncommon solution would be the right one. In our finished design, every space is lived in—and lived in regularly. Even primarily transitional areas are at the same time destinations in and of themselves. Weaknesses have been reinterpreted as strengths. I'm especially proud that we were able to look so far beyond what *was* there and perceive what *could be* there instead.

OPPOSITE: Charcoal-colored walls are a calming force in the cozy library, which serves as an entry to the primary bedroom suite. The console against the far wall is an old kneeler from a church; the pressed-tin retablos hung over it belonged to the client's mother and grandmother. Armchairs clad in black-and-cream ticking are a welcome place to read and decompress at the end of the day. **OVERLEAF:** In this house, too much is just enough.

THIS PAGE: People talk about "bringing the outdoors in," and typically they just mean windows and views. But we really did it in this house, with plants placed all over the back gallery and an assortment of welcoming furniture spilling out onto the rear terrace.
OPPOSITE: We designed the custom marble dining table specifically to go here. In lieu of a chandelier, we set mercury-glass candleholders into an iron plant hanger.
OVERLEAF: There is no rule that says outdoor furniture has to match. We made the exterior living space of this residence feel just as layered and bohemian as the inside.

A Frame for Beauty

As I mention in this book's introduction, the idea of beauty has deep emotional resonance for all of us. The pursuit of beauty is a worthy cause in and of itself—I believe that beauty can change the way we see ourselves and influence our lives for the better—and design is a means we use to get there. It's kind of like a fox hunt. You have to have the skills to ride, and the experience itself is exhilarating. But the goal, in the end, is to capture the fox. I use all of my design skills to go after the goal: beauty.

My clients for this project decided to move into a new house in a small, secluded neighborhood—a home that, although perfectly pleasant, was quite a bit more compact than the one they had just left, and whose interior spaces, although bright and open, were not especially distinguished. Since we weren't going to be building from the ground up, we had to work within the constraints of the existing layout (not that that stopped us from taking several areas, such as the kitchen, down to the studs). As always, we were looking to create genuine character, real depth—but we needed to do that more through recasting and refining aspects of the interiors than through major structural interventions.

We did shift one living room wall inward by about eighteen inches for better proportions (and were conveniently able to add some welcome square footage to the main bathroom suite in the process). The resulting reduced footprint in the living room allows the eye to be drawn upward, emphasizing the space's vertical dimension and, paradoxically, causing it to feel grander—almost more like a New York City apartment than like a typical house.

The family's truly magical collection of art and Spanish antiques, much of which has been handed down for generations, became the splendidly decorative core we planned around, conceiving every room as a low-key envelope to showcase a selection of exceptional pieces and let them shine. As a background foil for the home's pedigreed contents, we rigorously stripped away details from its inner architecture in favor of a quiet elegance.

OPPOSITE: "Spare yet striking" was the guiding principle for this house, which meant arriving at beauty via simple means. The club chair shown here had been passed down in the husband's family; we matched it with an extremely pared-down lamp and side table, then stationed the group beneath an abstract painting inherited by the wife.

OPPOSITE: Curtains screen the home's foyer from the living room beyond for a sense of mystery and discovery. **ABOVE:** The *bargueño* chest-on-stand in the foyer comes from the family's collection. A gilded lantern hangs low, as if you could carry it to light your way through the house. **OVERLEAF:** Sheer curtain "wings" give definition to the living room. Several fabrics employed here have the slightest of shell-pink undertones.

Main seating group beyond

Layers of sheers

Chaise as Room divider

Antique chairs in second grouping

Living Room

Small nail heads on ends

Large nail heads at base

Walnut legs

Leather on base

Mohair on cushions and bolsters

Romanza Chaise

One perfect example is the wall structure separating the living and family rooms. It's wrapped in white-lacquered millwork that neatly straddles the line between tradition and spare modernity: instead of raised moldings, narrow reveals delineate the panels for an effect that's nearly abstract without being jarringly contemporary. A see-through fireplace pierces the wall, surrounded in the more formal room by an absolutely smooth marble slab set flush into the surface. An equally pristine plate of darkened steel fulfills the same function on the opposite, more casual, side. Similar elements repeat elsewhere in the house for a consistent vibe.

In an environment with this degree of visual clarity, you have to be extra-judicious about what you put in, because each rug, light fixture, item of furniture, or decorative object has to count. Nothing that was only fair made the cut in here; it's totally an all-star lineup. Dramatic definition comes from a limited number of bold gestures positioned at strategic points. Carefully constructed arrangements frequently marry components that don't match but do have affinities of shape and style. The home reminds me of a piece of music where variations on a melody get passed around from one instrument to another.

As neutral as this residence may first appear to be, color plays a surprisingly important role in it, with delicate, barely there undertones of rose and gray blue animating the spaces. We added faintly pink-hued French limestone floors throughout except in the principal bath—a hugely helpful common thread for promoting coherence in a house of this size—and dashes of taupe, caramel, gold, silver, and even a lemony yellow green crop up as accents in different rooms.

Everything's textural here. You want to sink into every sofa, chaise, and club chair; the patina on a carved chest invites a caress. One particularly welcome facet of the project was getting to reuse so many old favorites from the clients' previous home to fashion them a compelling new one (although custom designs done specifically for this dwelling are naturally also part of the mix).

Overall, as in a work of minimalist art, success is achieved through precision. There's no hiding. The more obvious each brushstroke is, the more crucial the contribution that each one makes. Careful editing and a handful of dynamic moments set the tone. Some houses you walk into and they have fantastic atmosphere even when empty. This house, on the other hand, is all about using the right finishes, furnishings, and fixtures in the right way to *generate* atmosphere—turning the whole thing into a perfect display case for the family's very special treasures.

PAGE 204: We designed a custom daybed to divide the living room into separate seating groups. PAGE 205: A razor-thin reveal outlines the paneling around a flush marble fireplace. OPPOSITE: A medley of curved shapes, along with the simple contrast of lights and darks, helps the relatively small dining space really sing.

PRECEDING SPREAD: Every shelf and tabletop is an opportunity for loveliness. **RIGHT:** The kitchen was laid out with no upper cabinets so that it wouldn't feel crowded. Slab doors in a taupe cerused oak provide beautiful texture. The iron chandelier was brought over from the foyer of the couple's previous home. **OVERLEAF:** The family room is a sort of informal twin to the living room, with cooler colors and a relaxed vibe.

RIGHT: A floor-to-ceiling upholstered headboard and custom double nightstands lend the principal bedroom a sense of grandeur, while a subtle interplay of camel and silvery blue-gray shades infuses the overall neutral palette with an energy it wouldn't otherwise have.
OVERLEAF: Rectangles are a quiet but pervasive presence in this home.

ABOVE AND OPPOSITE: The guest suite makes me think of lemon sorbet covered in caramel sauce, and it doubles as a getaway for the couple, where he goes to read and she can indulge in a long soak. **OVERLEAF:** Like so much of this house, the back garden is all about editing and using distinctive gestures to set a tone.

Making it Personal

This ranch, which belongs to my wife's family, sits in the heart of the Texas Hill Country west of Austin, not far outside her hometown of Fredericksburg. The land—a gorgeous rolling patchwork of gnarled live oak trees laden with ball moss, grassy meadows dotted with Indian blanket and prairie coneflower (known locally as Mexican hats), and the occasional prickly pear cactus—was bought by her grandfather nearly a hundred years ago, in the 1930s. Spring-fed ponds empty into the meandering Pedernales River, and the primitive camp house on-site was a favorite retreat for several generations of the clan.

A few years ago, we designed the architecture and interiors for my in-laws' new main house. More recently, they decided to add a guest cottage on their property as well. In this instance, we chose a *Southern Living* cottage plan for the structure, which is small and rustic in style, a single floor plus an additional upstairs sleeping loft. It looks (and functions) in some ways like one of Fredericksburg's old "Sunday houses": compact, unassuming buildings that farm families used overnight when they came into town on the weekends for church.

A guesthouse, in my opinion, needs to be lighthearted and carefree, and even have a sense of humor. And I often had to laugh in the course of this project, because I was never sure if I was designing for my mother-in-law or for myself. Although the guesthouse was meant to accommodate extended family, the process was one of envisioning a getaway purely for Autumn and me: a comfortable, textural oasis where we can kick our feet up—restful, if not exactly in a Zen-spare way. Despite its diminutive size, there's a lot of stuff in it. It almost feels like an attic with all its contents spilled out

A major perk of the design life is that you tend to collect so many wonderful things. Certain pieces pass through your hands quickly, bought for a specific home or client. Other "leftover" items hang around, either in your own house or in storage. If they aren't used now, they will be later, sometimes repainted

OPPOSITE: This project is a favorite because it packs so much design punch into a snug little structure. In a vacation home, it's easy to be lighthearted and adventurous, to branch out more. As I like to remind clients, however, you can do that in your first home as well. **OVERLEAF:** The guesthouse sits on a little stone ridge that drops off toward a meadow on the other side, with more hills in the distance.

or reupholstered or otherwise adapted for new purposes and a new career. We outfitted this place accordingly with a lot of our own furniture. The downstairs bed had been made for us by a Hill Country craftsman long ago. The living room chaise is one that stood in our Austin family room for years, in front of the fireplace, and survived four children. We re-covered it in rich orange leather and mohair and set it right in front of the fireplace here.

Working on the guesthouse was a chance to empty out our closets *and* make something beautiful, and a rare occasion when we didn't have to get everything right the first go-round. There was room for experimentation. My favorite color is orange, which I don't use a lot in my work. Here, it's counterpointed with gray and brown and black. If you simply lay out swatches of these colors, they don't look great. Give them a judicious blend, though, and they feel like a ranch: they're ironwork, they're dirt, they're tree bark. The colors take their cues from where we are. I also don't do a lot of vintage, but I enjoyed giving this place a bit of a vintage modern tinge. The papier-mâché architectural ornaments on the living room's chimney breast play fun geometry games with the iron chandelier and the cantilevered coffee table. Pairing a Saarinen table in the dining room with odd chairs that are part Queen Anne, part twentieth-century office is really, I think, almost misbehaving slightly.

We wanted relaxed and approachable—that's one reason why we did unlined cotton window treatments and a concrete floor. At the same time, we wanted stylish—which is why the ticking stripes on the curtains rhyme with patterned pillows and vertical chair slats elsewhere in the rooms, and the concrete floor is stained the color of super-super-dark coffee. An element of humbleness that relates to the country surroundings is combined with a dose of chic that makes us happy.

Originally a major source of the family's livelihood, the ranch is still a hub where everyone gathers for big events such as Thanksgiving and Easter, when long tables get pulled out under the trees and a rope is slung over a branch to hold a chandelier. As we intended, the guesthouse provides visitors with a separate, tiny haven where they can decompress and take in the peace of the surrounding countryside. Charming, quirky, simple, yet with layer upon layer of design interest—just a perfect spot to practice gratitude, celebrate milestones, and enjoy the leftovers.

OPPOSITE: The living room furniture includes a pair of rattan chairs I got from an English antiques dealer in Austin, the gateleg table was bought at auction, and the hexagon-patterned hide rug has irregular edges that just sort of drift off in different directions. We picked up the iron flower on the cocktail table at a lovely little art store in Tel Aviv. **PAGES 228 AND 229:** We put a Saarinen table in the dining room under a mercury-glass lantern in order not to be too correct, plus two odd chairs we found at auction and a collection of vintage pewter and silver plate and white ceramics that I've been gathering forever.

- Kitchen Beyond
- Curtains flanking Kitchen Opening
- "Vintage" Refrigerator
- Saarenin Dining Table
- Chairs from Round Top
- Mercury Glass Lantern
- Black Concrete Floor

Secretary as bar and breakfast station

Restaurant style stainless counters.

Small scale Range

RIGHT: With so much going on in a really small space, it was important to use rhythm and the repetition of like shapes, colors, and materials to keep the total effect under control. And we simply had fun playing within the looser constraints of a guesthouse—for instance, a kitchen that didn't need to produce major meals could be outfitted with a secretary, a small freestanding range and refrigerator, and stainless-steel tables.

RIGHT: Black walls and ceiling and creamy draperies make a cocoon out of the main bedroom, with just enough gold accents to add some sparkle. I picked up the textile that covers the nightstand in the medina in Marrakech; the painting of river stones is by a local Hill Country artist.

OPPOSITE: Everything is low in the upstairs loft sleeping area—even the bed is on the floor, with beautiful fabrics draped over it. An old kneeler we found at Round Top serves as the headboard. **ABOVE:** The brass vase is fashioned from a World War I–era artillery shell. **OVERLEAF:** Family dinners under the live oaks happen around a long table that once stood in a dance hall Autumn's father owns. Embroidered burlap makes a rustic-chic tablecloth.

ACKNOWLEDGMENTS

As a guy who would rather sit for hours and tell someone why I appreciate them, it would take me more than half of the book to really cover all the people I want to thank here in writing. So I'll do my best with the space I have. First and foremost, huge thanks to the love of my life, my best friend and amazing business partner, Autumn. All things are better with you.

To my mom, for making home a beautiful and safe place that always called me back. To my dad, who during his lifetime was my biggest fan and a model of optimism, integrity, and hard work. And to them both, for demonstrating well that other "romance of home." To my kids, my brother, Monty, and my extended family for loving me and cheering me on.

To the community in my hometown, Orange, Texas, that invested in me for years: teachers, friends, families down the street, our church, and so on. And particularly to Nelson Nolden: "attention to detail," "results, not excuses," and "whatever it takes" are phrases I still use in my business.

Thanks for the relationships and influences that came from my time at Baylor University, especially to my college buddies and their families for being lifelong friends and fans. You know who you are. Sic 'em, Bears! And thanks to the mentors in Waco who gave me vision and initiative for life.

To all those who have been design inspirations during the journey: my aunt Sandy, for modeling joy in design; Micky Johnson and Anne Tiffany, for insisting that I go into design; in memory of Dorothy Shellenberger, for truly living with beauty and style; Carol and the late Tim Bolton, for teaching me to see differently; Annie Brudno, for sharing her wealth of knowledge; Howell Ridout, for championing details; and Marla Bommarito-Crouch, for personifying professionalism. To the men who have walked a few steps ahead and have been so generous with their wisdom, experience, and encouragement: Keith Granet, Grant Kirkpatrick, and Greg Tankersley.

To my amazing coworkers Stacie Grimes Bigott, Emily Fox, Maggie Wakefield, Robby Jenks, Kristal Trotty Hansen, Erin Schneider, and Camden Michalek, who put their hearts and souls into the projects—this book is as much yours as mine. A special thanks to Kadra Johnson, for all of your love and support.

Thank you to Pedro and Mary Katherine Alonso, for taking a risk before I even had a portfolio. And great thanks to all the clients who have invited us into their houses and lives. A special thanks for those who let us include their homes here.

Thanks to the entire team who made this book possible: Jill Cohen, for inspiration and vision; Lizzy Hyland and Rizzoli editor Sandra Gilbert Freidus, for shepherding that vision; Doug Turshen and David Huang, for their amazing book-design talent; and Kyle Hoepner, for taking my ideas and crafting them into warm and engaging words.

My gratitude to those who helped create the gorgeous images in this book: Lisa Romerein—you are a great "dance partner" and friend. To Peter Vitale, for your insight and camaraderie. Thanks as well to Dean Courtois, Andrew Petrich, and Harry Greiner, for the heavy lifting and for making the shoots happen. To Robin Turk and Eleanor Roper, for their impeccable styling and imagination.

And, lastly, thanks to the God of the universe for unending grace and the gift of creativity.

OPPOSITE: I designed this custom blackened-steel candlestand for a family's private chapel.

ARTIST CREDITS
All watercolors by Marcus Mohon

Rufino Tamayo, *Hambreen Rosa*, 1984
Artwork © 2024 Tamayo Heirs / Mexico /
Artists Rights Society (ARS), New York
Pages 20, 25

Rufino Tamayo, *El Person*, 1975
Artwork © 2024 Tamayo Heirs / Mexico /
Artists Rights Society (ARS), New York
Page 21

Andy Warhol, *Details of Renaissance Paintings*
(*Leonardo da Vinci, The Annunciation, 1472*), 1984
Artwork © 2024 The Andy Warhol Foundation
for the Visual Arts, Inc. / Licensed by Artists Rights
Society (ARS), New York
Page 47

Alex Katz, *Departure*, 2017
Artwork © 2024 Alex Katz / Licensed by VAGA
at Artists Rights Society (ARS), New York
Pages 128, 133

Donald Sultan, *Morning Glories December 10, 2002*, 2002
Artwork © 2024 Donald Sultan / Artists Rights Society
(ARS), New York
Page 142

Pablo Picasso, *Peintre et Modele IV*, 1963
Artwork © 2024 Estate of Pablo Picasso /
Artists Rights Society (ARS), New York
Page 144

Luis Jiménez, *Drawing for Progress I*, 1973
Artwork © 2024 Luis A. Jimenez, Jr. Copyright Trust /
Artists Rights Society (ARS), New York
Page 179

Henri Matisse, *Danseuse allongée, Tête accoudée,
from Dix Danseuses* (*Lying Dancer, Head Resting,
from Ten Dancers*), 1925–1926
Artwork © 2024 Succession H. Matisse /
Artists Rights Society (ARS), New York
Page 205

PHOTOGRAPHY CREDITS
Lisa Romerein: front cover, pages 2–3, 5, 6, 10, 13, 17–37,
40–49, 51–61, 64–71, 73, 75–85, 88, 89, 91, 94–99, 101–111,
114, 115, 117–125, 148–153, 155–165, 186–190, 192, 193, 195,
196–197, 200–203, 205, 207–221, 224–225, 227–237, 239,
back cover

Stephen Karlisch: page 4

Peter Vitale: pages 128–129, 132, 133, 135–137,
139–145, 168–169, 172, 174–183

ARCHITECTURE CREDITS
Sanctuary and Taken Away: Charles Travis
New Life and A Sheltered Place: Gary Koerner
Belonging: Michael G. Imber
Imparting Identity: Weldon Turner
Making It Personal: William H. Phillips

PAGE 5: In this powder room, dogwood branches
rhyme gorgeously with the veins in a marble
backsplash. PAGE 6: Custom doors and sconces,
plus an antique bench, combine to make a stairway
magical. PAGE 10: An easygoing assembly of art and
objects sets the tone for an Austin residence.

First published in the United States of America in 2025 by
Rizzoli International Publications, Inc.
49 West 27th Street
New York, NY 10001
www.rizzoliusa.com

Copyright © 2025 Mohon Interiors
Copyright © 2025 watercolors by Marcus Mohon

Publisher: Charles Miers
Project Editor: Sandra Gilbert Freidus
Design: Doug Turshen with David Huang
Production Manager: Barbara Saddick
Managing Editor: Lynn Scrabis
Editorial Assistance: Hilary Ney, Kelli Rae Patton, and
Rachel Selekman

Developed in collaboration with Jill Cohen Associates, LLC

Printed in China

2025 2026 2027 2028 / 10 9 8 7 6 5 4 3 2 1

ISBN: 978-0-8478-4644-3
Library of Congress Control Number: 2024946659

Visit us online:
Instagram.com/RizzoliBooks
Facebook.com/RizzoliNewYork
X: @Rizzoli_Books
Youtube.com/user/RizzoliNY

Tapered Arm

Cover in back

Bench Seat

End
pillow?

Walnut
leg

Sofa
study